Get to Know Wheels and Axles

by Paul Challen

Crabtree Publishing Company

www.crabtreebooks.com

Crabtree Publishing Company
www.crabtreebooks.com

Author: Paul Challen
Editors: Molly Aloian, Reagan Miller, Crystal Sikkens
Project coordinator: Robert Walker
Prepress technicians: Ken Wright, Margaret Amy Salter
Production coordinator: Margaret Amy Salter
Cover design: Samara Parent
Coordinating editor: Chester Fisher
Series and project editor: Penny Dowdy
Project manager: Kumar Kunal (Q2AMEDIA)
Art direction: Dibakar Acharjee (Q2AMEDIA)
Design: Tarang Saggar (Q2AMEDIA)
Photo research: Farheen Aadil (Q2AMEDIA)

Illustrations:
Rob MacGregor: page 28
Q2AMedia Art Bank: pages 6, 7, 8, 10, 11, 14, 15,
  16, 17, 18, 19, 22, 23, 26, 27

Photographs:
123RF: p. 29
Corbis: Hulton-Deutsch Collection: p. 9 ;
Dreamstime: Newphotose: p. 21
Ingram photo objects: p. 4 (lever)
Istockphoto: page 20; Clayton Hansen:
  p. 4 (wheel and axle), 31; David Freund:
  p. 13; Valerie Loiseleux: p. 24; Michael Banks:
  p. 25 (wheel)
Shutterstock: Medvedev Andrey: p. 4 (screw);
  Andrjuss: p. 4 (wedge); Julián Rovagnati:
  p. 4 (inclined plane); Harley Molesworth:
  p. 4 (pulley); Alex Melnick: p. 5; Luisa Fernanda
  Gonzalez: p. 12; Timothy Large: p. 25 (road)

Library and Archives Canada Cataloguing in Publication

Challen, Paul, 1967-
  Get to know wheels and axles / Paul Challen.

(Get to know simple machines)
Includes index.
ISBN 978-0-7787-4471-9 (bound).--ISBN 978-0-7787-4488-7 (pbk.)

    1. Wheels--Juvenile literature. 2. Axles--Juvenile literature.
I. Title. II. Series: Get to know simple machines

TJ181.5.C43 2009   j621.8   C2009-900811-4

Library of Congress Cataloging-in-Publication Data

Challen, Paul C. (Paul Clarence), 1967-
  Get to know wheels and axles / Paul Challen.
    p. cm. -- (Get to know simple machines)
  Includes index.
  ISBN 978-0-7787-4488-7 (pbk. : alk. paper) -- ISBN 978-0-7787-4471-9
(reinforced library binding : alk. paper)
  1. Wheels--Juvenile literature. 2. Axles--Juvenile literature. I. Title. II. Series.

TJ147.C45 2009
621.8--dc22

                                    2009004588

Crabtree Publishing Company
www.crabtreebooks.com   1-800-387-7650   Printed in the U.S.A./112012/JA20121109

Published in Canada
Crabtree Publishing
616 Welland Ave.
St. Catharines, ON
L2M 5V6

Published in the United States
Crabtree Publishing
PMB 59051
350 Fifth Avenue, 59th Floor
New York, New York 10118

Published in the United Kingdom
Crabtree Publishing
Maritime House
Basin Road North, Hove
BN41 1WR

Published in Australia
Crabtree Publishing
3 Charles Street
Coburg North
VIC, 3058

Contents

What is a Simple Machine?

All people have jobs to do. Some jobs take a lot of **energy**. Energy is the ability to do work. Simple machines help people get jobs done without working too hard. This is called **mechanical advantage**.

Simple machines are tools that are made up of very few parts. There are six kinds of simple machines. They are inclined planes, levers, pulleys, wedges, screws, and **wheels** and **axles**.

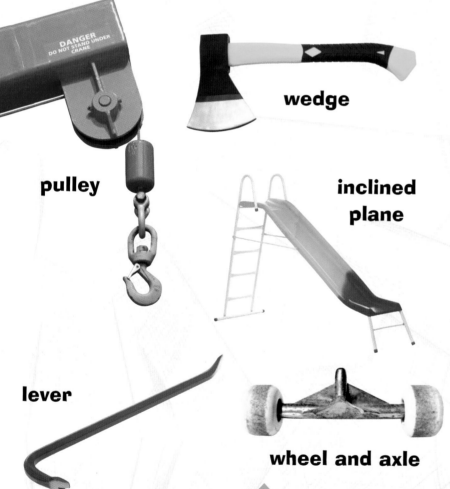

pulley

wedge

inclined plane

lever

wheel and axle

screw

These pictures show an example of each kind of simple machine.

One kind of simple machine is a wheel and axle. A wheel and axle is a wheel or set of wheels that is connected to a bar. A wheel and axle is used to move objects or change the speedor direction of a moving object.

Wheels and axles are used all around you. You can see them on door knobs, cars, and ferris wheels.

The Basic Design

This activity will show you how a basic wheel and axle is made. You will need:

drinking straw

2 circles cut from a cardboard box (must be fairly thick)

Have an adult poke a hole in the center of each circle. Push the straw into the cardboard.

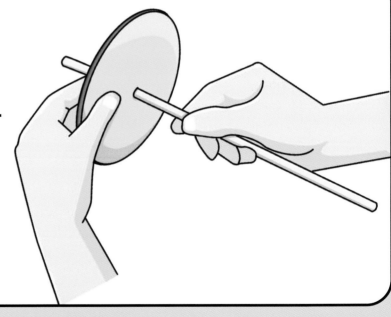

Make the same attachment with the other cardboard circle at the other end of the straw.

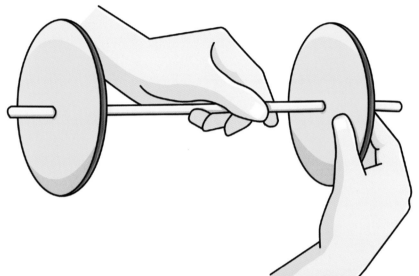

The straw is the axle. The cardboard circles are the wheels.

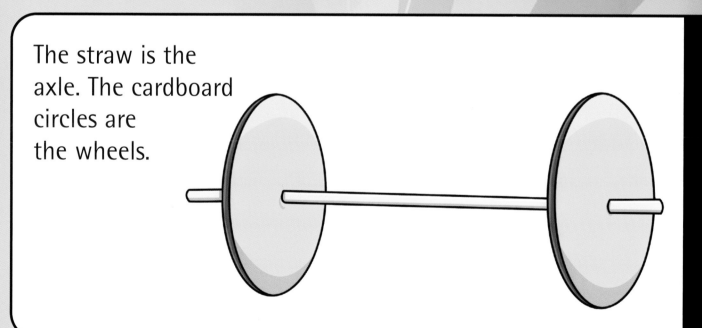

How it Works

The wheel and axle makes it easier to move objects. The wheel and axle is one of the oldest inventions. Humans first used wheels and axles more than 5,000 years ago.

A wheel is made up of a circular frame and spokes, or simply a solid, round disk. An axle is a straight, solid object. A wheel attaches to the axle, and spins around it in a movement called **rotation**. The axle can rotate, making the wheel rotate, too. You can put more than one wheel on an axle. If the axle rotates, all the wheels on it will rotate, too.

Axles can have more than one wheel.

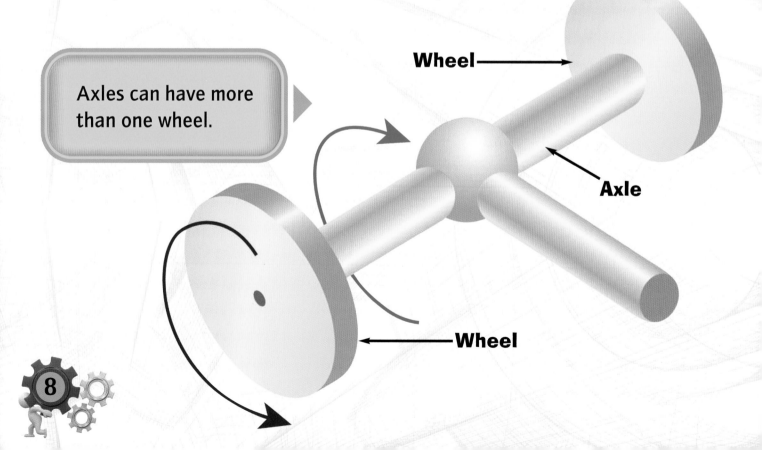

Wheel

Axle

Wheel

How different is this old-fashioned car than ones used today?

Cars and trucks use wheels made of rubber and axles made of metal. This design has not changed very much in the last 100 years.

Round and Round

This activity will show you how a wheel and an axle work together. You will need:

drinking straw

2 circles cut from a cardboard box (must be fairly thick)

Step 1

Use the straw and cardboard construction you built on pages 6-7.

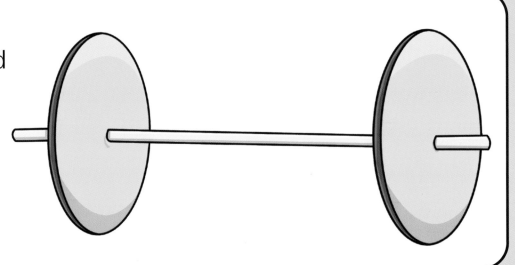

Roll the straw.
You will notice
how the cardboard
circles also rotate.

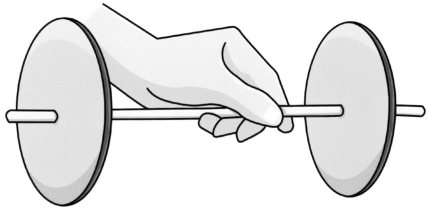

Hold the straw loosely in
one hand. With your other
hand, turn one
wheel. You will
notice how the
axle and the
other wheel
also rotates.

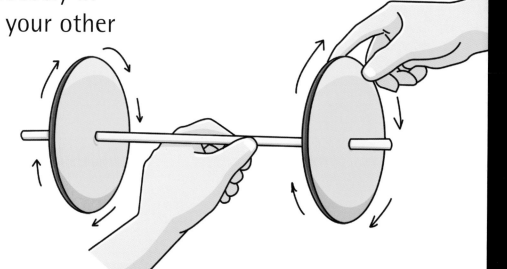

Moving Loads

You can attach an object such as a board or a basket onto a wheel and axle. Imagine that you placed a load on the board or in the basket. The wheel and axle will make this load much easier to carry than dragging it.

A very basic example of this is a pushcart. A pushcart is a large container with handles attached to a wheel and axle. Pushcarts make moving a load easy because the movement of the wheels spreads out the load over a distance. It uses less energy to move the load.

Moving a load using a pushcart is much easier than dragging the load on the ground.

How many wheels does this truck use to carry its load?

A transport truck is a great example of wheels and axles moving a load. Many transport trucks have several axles and many wheels.

A Multi-Axle Model

This activity will show you how multiple wheels and axles work together. You will need:

tape

3 drinking straws

6 cardboard disks

A piece of strong cardboard about 3 inches (7.5 cm) wide and 12 inches (30 cm) long

paper clips

coins

Step 1

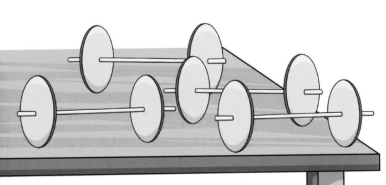

Use the wheel-and-axle construction from pages 6-7. Build three more of the same wheel-and-axle sets.

Put the four axles in a
row. Place the cardboard
under the axles. Tape
the cardboard
to each axle.
Turn it over.

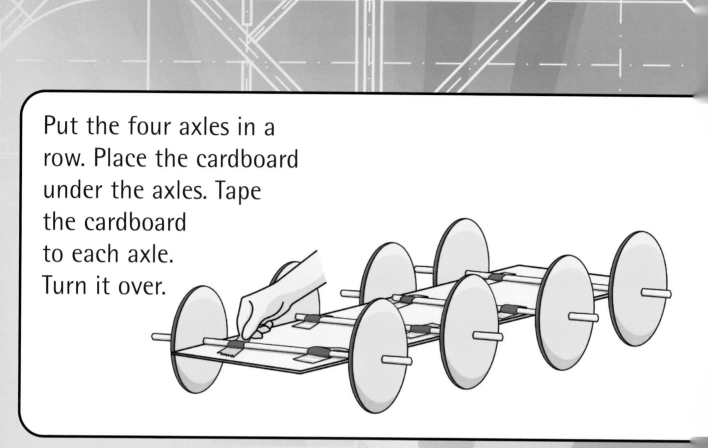

Put the paper clips, coins, or other
small objects on top of the cardboard.
Push the model forward. You will see
how this multi-wheeled vehicle moves
your load.

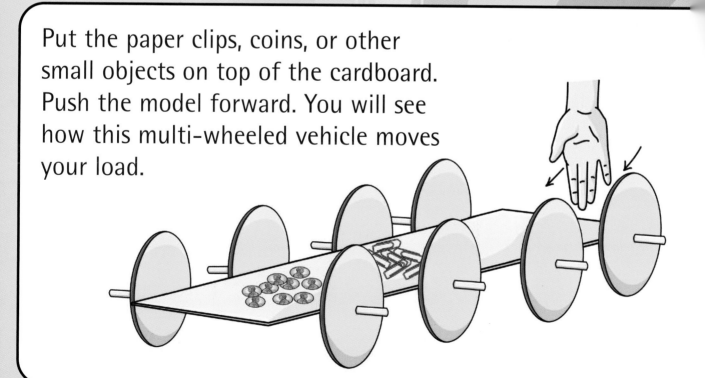

A Lifting Machine

Wheels make it easier to carry loads over a long distance. Wheels can also help us lift objects. Think about how a well works. The top of the well has a wheel with a handle. That wheel is attached to an axle. A rope is attached to the axle.

If you turn the handle, the wheel and axle will make the rope go up or down. When you put a bucket at the end of the rope, the bucket will go up or down in the well. This makes it a great tool for lifting water.

A wheel and axle can make lifting water a lot easier.

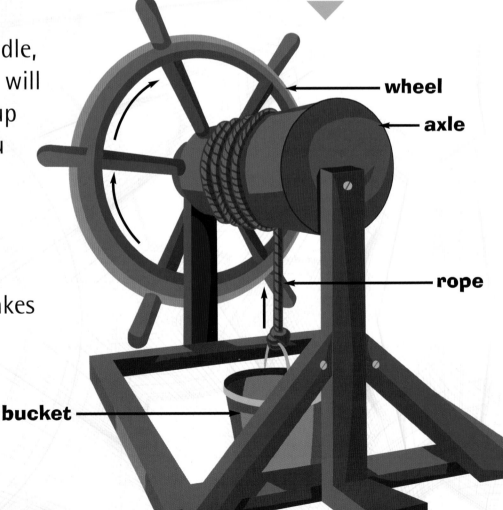

wheel

axle

rope

bucket

This is called a set of wheels.

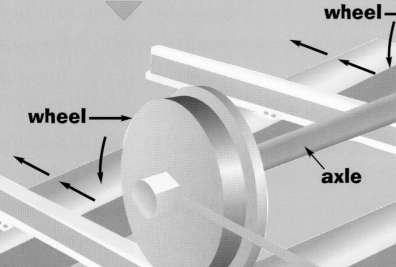

wheel

wheel

axle

track

When two wheels are attached to one axle, and placed on a track so that both wheels travel at the same time and in the same direction, it is called a set of wheels.

Build a Lifting Machine

This activity will show you how a lifting machine uses a wheel and axle. You will need:

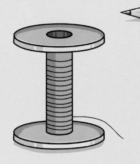

a spool of string

a long pencil

some paper clips

Place the pencil inside the spool so the spool can rotate around it.

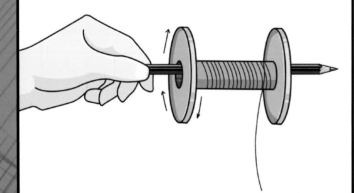

Unroll a little bit of the string and attach a paper clip to it.

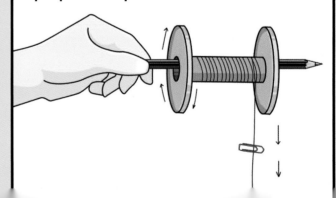

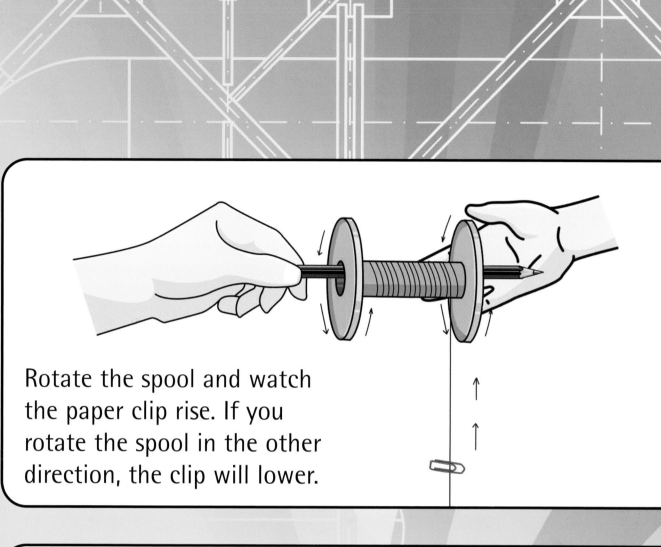

Rotate the spool and watch the paper clip rise. If you rotate the spool in the other direction, the clip will lower.

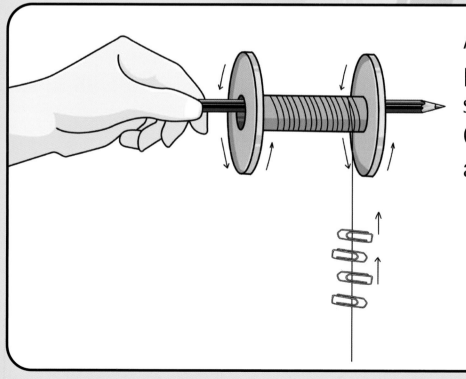

Attach as many paperclips as the string can hold. Can the wheel and axle lift the load?

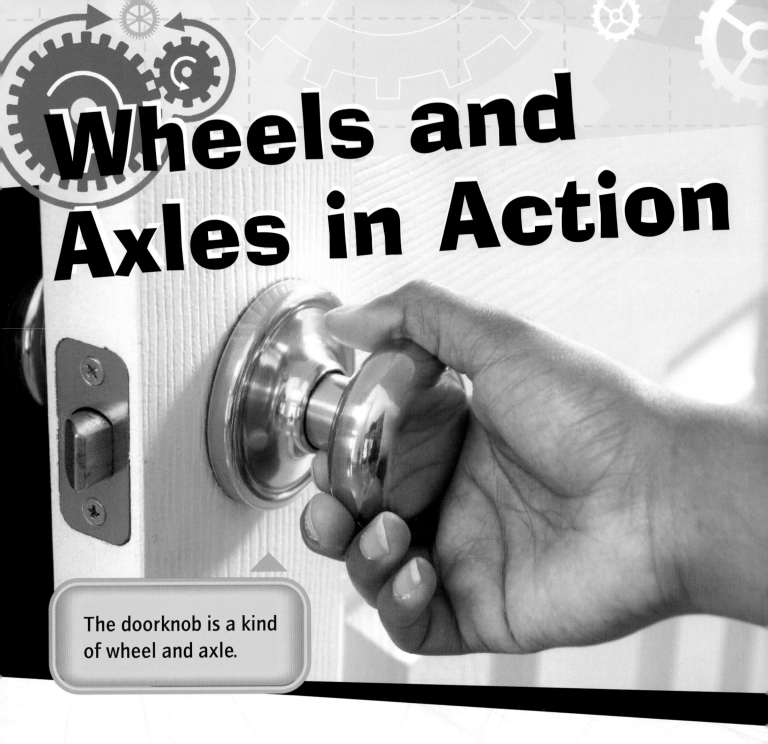

Wheels and Axles in Action

The doorknob is a kind of wheel and axle.

We usually think of the wheel and axle as a simple machine found on cars, bicycles, or roller skates. But a wheel and axle can be any object that uses an axle in the center of a circular object.

Think of a round doorknob as a "wheel," attached to a rod or axle that goes inside the door. When the knob is rotated, it turns the rod, which is attached to a latch that opens it.

20

Where are the wheel and axle located on a faucet?

The faucet is a wheel-and-axle simple machine. The circular faucet handle is a wheel that opens and closes. It turns a valve (the axle) that controls the water flow.

The Fan in Action

This activity shows how a fan uses the wheel-and-axle design. You will need:

spool

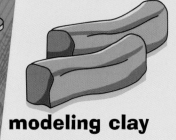

modeling clay

a long pencil

2 or 3 straws

construction paper

tape

Stand the spool on a table.

Put the pencil (the axle) through the center of the spool (the wheel). You may need to add the modeling clay to the spool's center to make the pencil fit tightly. When the pencil rotates, the spool should rotate too.

Cut the straws in half. Use the modeling clay, to attach four to six spokes to the outside of the spool. The more spokes you put on the wheel, the more blades the fan will have.

Fold a piece of construction paper over each spoke. Tape it closed to completely cover the straw. These are your fan blades.

Rotate the pencil slowly and watch the fan blades turn. Increase the speed of your axle (the pencil) and feel the increased wind from the fan!

Fighting Friction

Friction is the force created when one object rubs against another object. For example, rub your hands together quickly. Do your hands feel hot? The heat you feel is caused by friction!

When you drag something along a surface, it creates friction. If there is a lot of friction, you could damage the object you are dragging. When you move something with a wheel and axle, you create much less friction than if you drag it. The wheels turn smoothly over the surface.

Dragging this bag of leaves along the ground causes friction. Friction can make work more difficult and take more time.

The skid marks are made by the friction between a tire and the road.

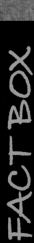

FACT BOX

When a car stops suddenly, the wheels stop rotating and they slide along the road. This creates a lot of friction. Rubber from the tires sticks to the road, making skid marks!

Creating Friction

This activity will show you how friction is created. You will need:

a toy car

tape

Step 1

Roll the car back and forth over the desk quickly. Touch the bottom of the wheels. They should feel cool.

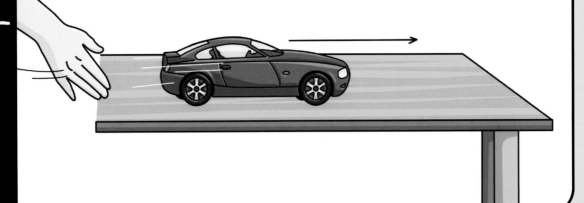

Now, tape all four wheels so they cannot turn.

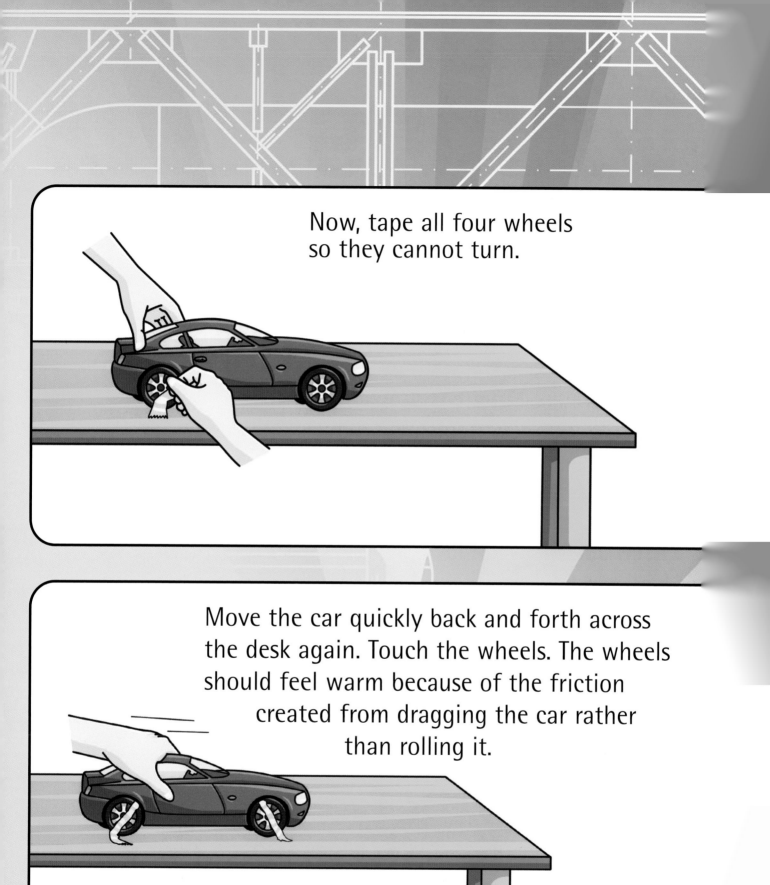

Move the car quickly back and forth across the desk again. Touch the wheels. The wheels should feel warm because of the friction created from dragging the car rather than rolling it.

Working Together

When a simple machine such as the wheel and axle works together with other simple machines, they form a **complex machine**. There are hundreds of examples of wheels and axles working with levers, inclined planes, and wedges to form complex machines.

A great example of a complex machine is the **bicycle**. Bikes use wheels and axles to move, and they also use levers to steer (the handlebars), to stop (the brakes), and to park (the kickstand). Pedals are another type of lever, used to make bikes move forward and move faster or slower.

Can you spot the simple machines on this bike?

The penny farthing was a bicycle that was popular more than 100 years ago. It had a huge front wheel and a tiny back wheel. It was very hard to control!

Imagine trying to control this bike!

Glossary

axle A straight, solid object which rotates to spin a wheel, or which a wheel rotates around

bicycle A complex machine made up of wheels and axles and other simple machines

complex machine A machine made up of two or more simple machines

energy The ability to do work

friction A force pushing against two objects in contact with one another when at least one of them is moving

mechanical advantage The advantage created by a simple machine that helps people do a job using less energy

rotation The spinning motion of a wheel around an axle

simple machine A tool that makes work easier by spreading out the effort needed to move a load

wheel An object made up of a circular frame and spokes, or simply a solid round disk, that rotates on an axle

Index

Web sites

www.thinkquest.org/library (Type "wheels and axles" in the search box)

encarta.msn.com/encyclopedia_761562392/wheel_and_axle.html

inventors.about.com/od/wstartinventions/a/wheel.htm

www.mikids.com/SMachinesWheels.htm

www.education.com/activity/article/Wheel_And_Axle/